First published 2023
by Walker Books Ltd
87 Vauxhall Walk
London SE11 5HJ

This edition published 2025

2 4 6 8 10 9 7 5 3

© 1987–2025 Martin Handford

The right of Martin Handford to be identified as author of this work has been asserted in accordance with the Copyright, Designs and Patents Act 1988

EU Authorized Representative: HackettFlynn Ltd 36 Cloch Choirneal, Balrothery, Co. Dublin, K32 C942, Ireland. EU@walkerpublishinggroup.com

This book has been typeset in Wallyfont and Optima

Printed in China

All rights reserved. No part of this book may be reproduced, transmitted or stored in an information retrieval system in any form or by any means, graphic, electronic or mechanical, including photocopying, taping and recording, without prior written permission from the publisher. Additionally, no part of this book may be used or reproduced in any manner for the purpose of training artificial intelligence technologies or systems, nor for text and data mining.

British Library Cataloguing in Publication Data: a catalogue record for this book is available from the British Library

ISBN 978-1-5295-2391-1

www.walker.co.uk

WALKER BOOKS
AND SUBSIDIARIES
LONDON · BOSTON · SYDNEY · AUCKLAND

HI, WALLY-WATCHERS!

JOIN ME ON AN AWESOME JOURNEY OF A LIFETIME, PACKED WITH TERRIFIC TRIPS AND HEAPS OF SURPRISES!

WHAT'S MORE, WHEREVER WE VISIT THERE'S A MIND-BOGGLING MAZE WITH OODLES OF TWISTS AND TURNS TO MAKE US DIZZY! TACKLE EACH MAZE BY TRACING YOUR FINGER FROM START TO FINISH, BUT BE WARNED: IT'S EASIER SAID THAN DONE!

ALONG THE WAY, I'LL CHALLENGE YOU TO EXPLORE EXTRA ROUTES WITH LOTS OF THINGS TO FIND. TURN LEFT, BEAR RIGHT, GO STRAIGHT AHEAD OR ROUND AND ROUND, AND BE PREPARED TO DOUBLE BACK ON YOURSELF, TOO. IF YOU END UP WHERE YOU STARTED, JUST SET OFF AGAIN!

OH, AND LOOK OUT FOR ME AND MY SIGHTSEEING PALS IN EVERY SCENE: WOOF (BUT ALL YOU CAN SEE IS HIS TAIL), WENDA, WIZARD WHITEBEARD AND ODLAW. CAN YOU ALSO SPOT OUR LOST THINGS: MY KEY, WOOF'S BONE, WENDA'S CAMERA, WIZARD WHITEBEARD'S SCROLL AND ODLAW'S BINOCULARS?

GET READY TO BE A-MAZE-D!

Wally

A MINI-MAZE WARM-UP!

Before you set off on your journey, try diving into this map! Trace a route from **START** to **FINISH** avoiding the hats that have been dropped along the way. Complete each mini-maze as you reach it by working from **x** to **★**. Finally, plot a path starting from each character to reunite them with their matching headwear (you may cross over other hats to do this!). Good luck!

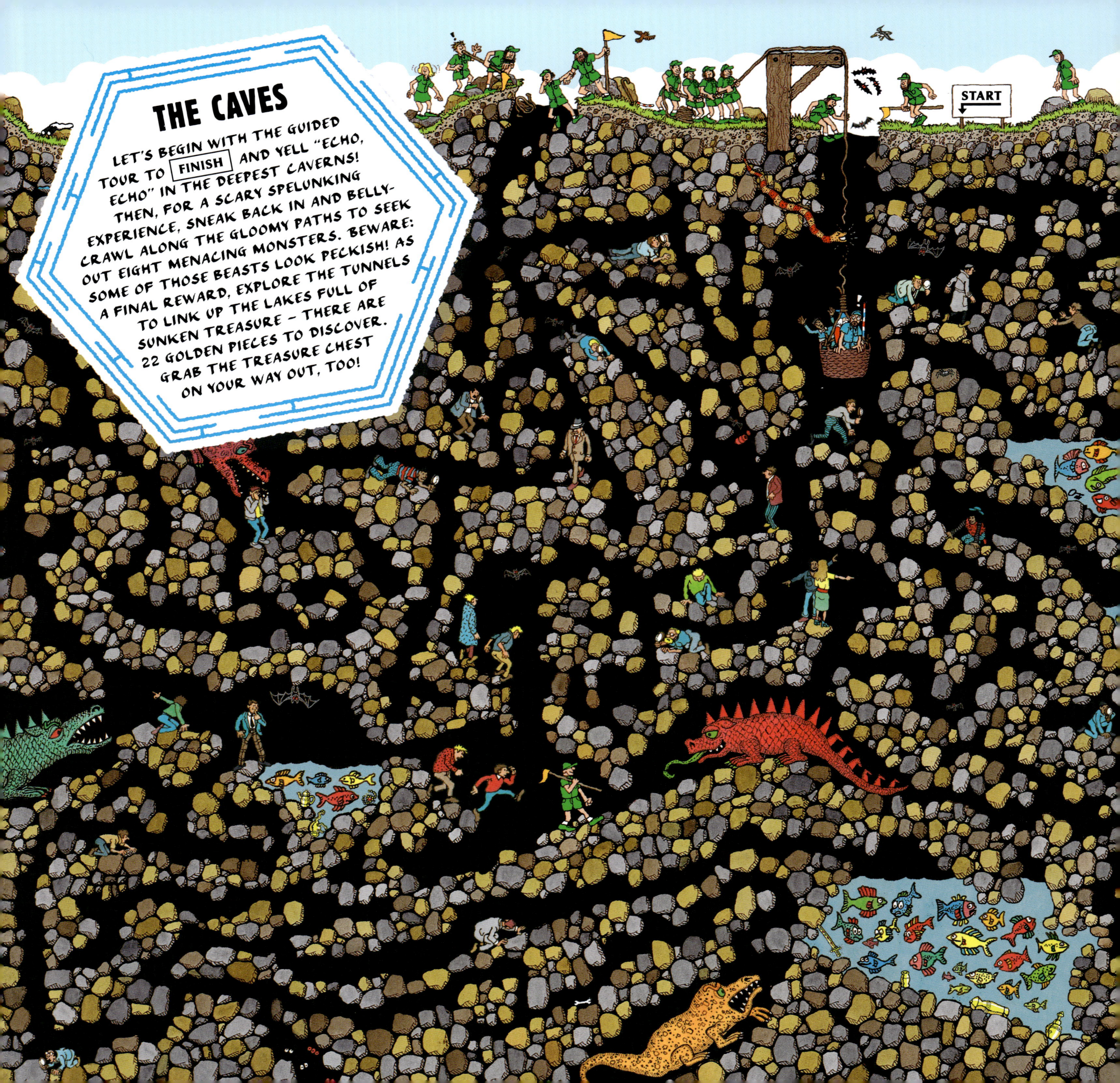

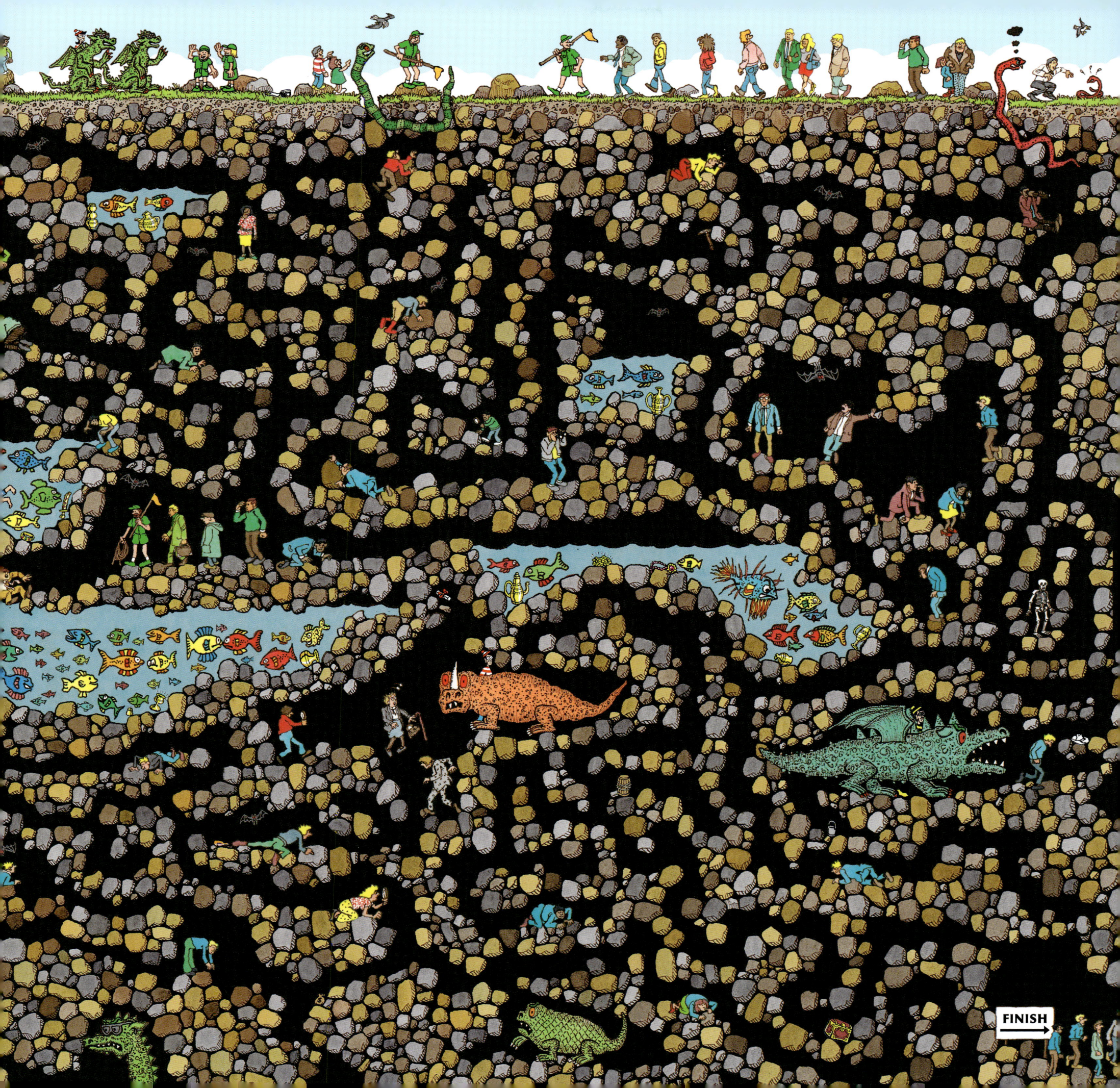

START

WHERE'S WALLY?
A-MAZE-ING JOURNEYS

CHECKLISTS
Now it's time to take a trip down memory lane! Return to all the amazing places on this journey and search for the many wonderful things in these checklists.

ONE LAST THING!
Dropped in one of the scenes is a tiny maze on a small piece of paper. Can you find it? See if you can complete the maze, too! You could use a magnifying glass to help.

THE CHATEAU GARDEN
- [ ] An electric fan
- [ ] A conga line
- [ ] An upside-down sedan chair
- [ ] A king
- [ ] Two women fencing
- [ ] A cat
- [ ] A ginormous glove
- [ ] A chequered flag
- [ ] Two violins
- [ ] A man wearing a sling

THE AIRPORT
- [ ] Runway runners
- [ ] A flying fish
- [ ] A bunch of balloons
- [ ] A telephone
- [ ] A UFO
- [ ] A windsock
- [ ] Two cows
- [ ] A queue of elephants
- [ ] A girl wearing a red-checked dress
- [ ] A fork-lift truck

THE SWEET FACTORY
- [ ] A person wearing a chicken headdress
- [ ] A tea party
- [ ] A juggler
- [ ] A person hugging a teddy bear
- [ ] Four jellies
- [ ] A skateboarder
- [ ] A person wearing a stripy scarf
- [ ] A swing
- [ ] A person holding a spanner
- [ ] A diver

THE MUSEUM
- [ ] A trumpet
- [ ] Two people doing handstands
- [ ] A globe
- [ ] A bike with square wheels
- [ ] A bag of golf clubs
- [ ] A clothes hanger
- [ ] A worried fish
- [ ] Two roller skates
- [ ] A lyre
- [ ] A skeleton riding a skeleton

WALLYWOOD FILM STUDIOS
- [ ] A suit of armour
- [ ] A Viking
- [ ] Frankenstein's monster
- [ ] A small snake
- [ ] A robot sipping on a straw
- [ ] A child on a space hopper
- [ ] Two joined hats
- [ ] A man with his foot in a bucket
- [ ] A boxer
- [ ] A banana costume

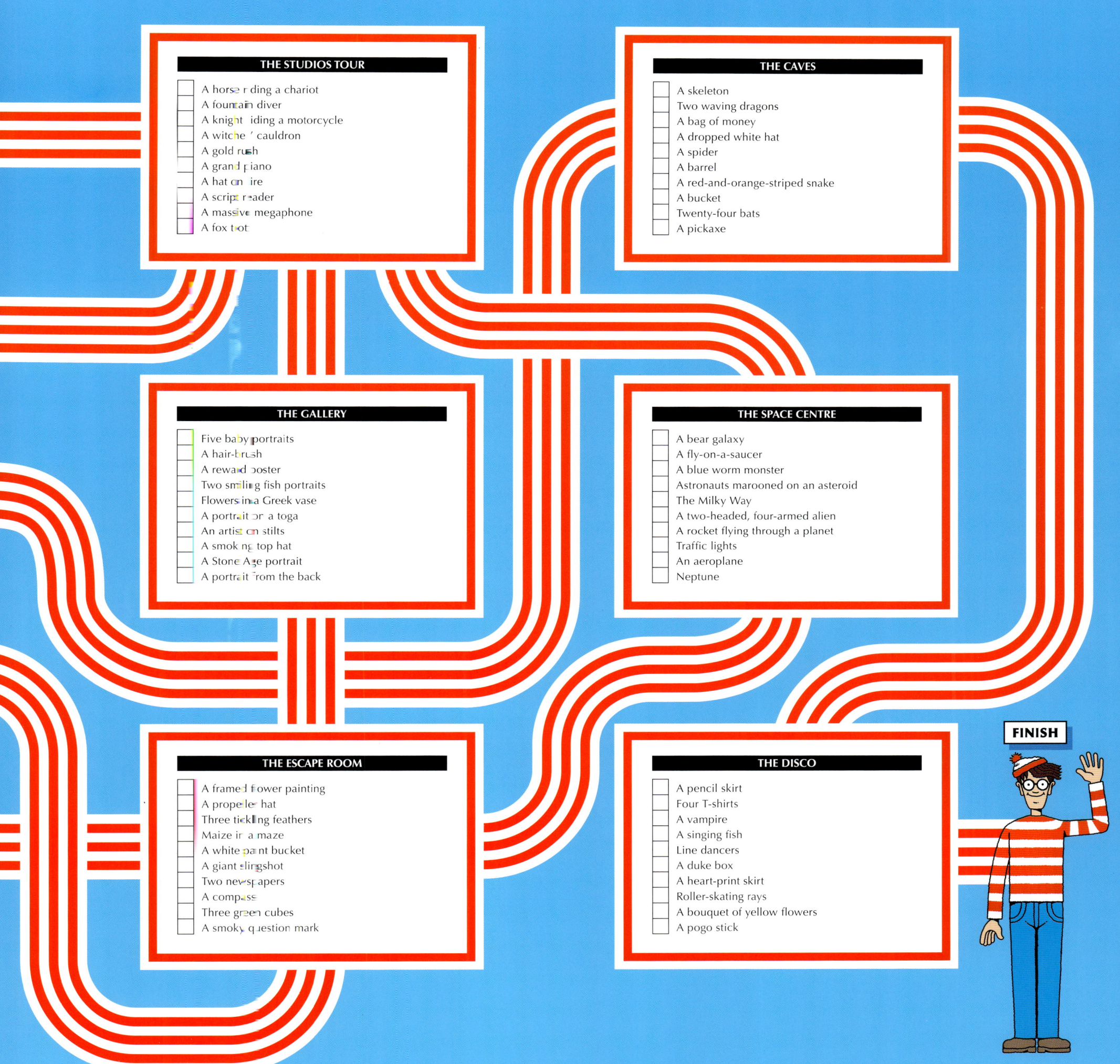